The Anti-Elevator Speech

Second Edition

By Cliff Suttle

Published by Suttle Enterprises, LLC
Novi, Michigan

ISBN: 978-0-578-03752-3

Printed in the US by InstantPublisher.com

To find out more about the author and other products and services visit their web-site at www.ExciteYourAudience.Com

Chapter One
Ah Ha!

Why did I decide to write this book? This is the single most important question you should ask yourself about any author of any book when deciding if you want to read their book. Your time is valuable. In truth, it's the only thing you really have in life, your time. Time is precious and something you don't want to waste. Therefore, what was my motivation behind sharing the information in this book with you? And, why should you care?

Let me share with you the events that lead to my decision to write the Anti-Elevator Speech book. One cold, Michigan winter day in January, I was at my desk setting up the details for my next seminar, when my wife Marilyn, tossed a flyer for a networking event right on top of my computer keyboard. That is her way of letting me know she thinks this is important. It is also a little on the annoying side, but sometimes that's the only way to get my attention. As I began reading the flyer, the networking event sounded good. It was being run by a group of not-for-profit organizations who help start up companies get off the ground. I have always liked encouraging people in my seminars to become entrepreneurs, so that caught my attention right off the bat. The event appeared to be a well run event and was properly promoted. Sure, what the heck,

I wasn't busy that night anyway. It sounded like fun. I always love a chance to meet new people, especially like-minded people, being that I am an entrepreneur myself.

On the night of the event, I walked into the beautiful facilities and found they even had some decent food. Always a plus. I've always lived by the rule, if you feed them, they'll come. Obviously, the people running this event felt the same way. There was about a hundred and fifty to two hundred people milling around some advertising booths, but the big buzz of the night was the finals of the elevator speech competition. It seemed to be on everyone's minds. I had never heard of such a thing myself, but I figured people will compete at just about anything, so why not elevator speeches.

If you're not familiar with elevator speeches, let me take a few moments to explain the concept. An elevator speech is a preplanned narrative about your company or product that is designed to share as much information as possible in a minute or two. If you have a chance meeting with a business contact, you can go straight into the elevator speech which will convey all the information they need to know.

However, knowing what I know about elevator speeches and how they are not that effective, I didn't give the competition much thought. I simply moved on with the business of networking. After all, that was the reason I was there in the first place. A businesswomen I knew, Sara, was at the event. She had seen me succeed at a number of speech competitions in the past, but not an elevator speech competition. The competitions Sara had seen me compete in were about motivational speaking. Sara knew I was a good speaker, which lead her to jump to some incorrect conclusions.

> "Are you competing in the finals of the elevator speech contest," Sara asked.

> "No, I wouldn't be able to compete in an elevator speech contest. I don't believe in them."

> "What??? You don't have an elevator speech?"

> "Nope."

> "Don't you like to network?"

> "Oh, I love to network. I have already talked to about a third of the people in the room who have asked me to share information about my company for at least five minutes and then asked for a business card."

> "Whoa, that's way better than I'm doing. How do you do that?"

While I was sharing the Reader's Digest version of my system with Sara, a number of other people overheard me and joined in the conversation. I spent the better part of a half hour describing my system to at least twenty people. I was getting a kick out of people trying out the system with their business model and products. It's an easy system to learn so people were picking up on the concept pretty fast.

My group conversation was interrupted by a commanding voice over the intercom directing us to take our seats in the auditorium. It was time for the main event, complete with a master of ceremonies, opening speakers and plenty of awards and accolades. The highlight, if you can call it that, of the evening was the elevator speech competition. The premise of the competition was simple. The competitors were pretending to stand in line at a donut shop. By chance, an imaginary, big time venture capitalist, portrayed by the master of ceremonies, was standing right behind them in line. They had to turn around and give their elevator pitch to this investor. The competitors would then be judged on how well they conveyed their message.

This was hard for me to sit through. Each competitor gave a scripted, three minute speech that sounded like the teacher in a Charlie Brown cartoon. You remember, where you could hear Charlie Brown talking, but the teacher just sounded like, "wah-wah-wah-wah," and you couldn't tell what she was saying. It wasn't long before each of these speeches turned into wah-wah-wah from the sheer, mind numbing boredom of it. These speeches were too long, too detailed, and not interesting to anyone patiently waiting in line for a Crispy Creme and cup of coffee. The winner was plausible at best. These scripted speeches may work in a sit down, formally scheduled, pitch meeting, but in a network-ing situation or chance meeting they were a disaster. If someone had started giving me one of these pitches, I would have left the donut shop and gone to get an Egg McMuffin, and I love donuts.

After the contest, there was another short networking session. People from all over the room were seeking me out to get more details about my method. After having seen the competitors, who had practiced and been professionally coached by top name business consultants, they were shocked at how much easier and more engaging my system was. They all wanted to know more. At least two of them were using the system fairly well before the end of the evening.

Was that the moment I decided to write this book? Nope. It actually happened about a week after the competition at a smaller, more intermate networking environment. There were less than twenty people at this event. The first person I met was a nice young woman from a business marketing company who immediately stuffed a flyer in my face. I thought to myself, "poor thing, she just doesn't get it. If only there was a book I could give her ..." BING! That was the moment. I suddenly had nightmarish flash backs to the elevator speech competition and to the smiles on the faces of the people who learned my system that night. It became very clear to me what I had to do.

I had information that people wanted and needed. This information could better their lives or at least their business lives. Who was I to keep it to myself. I knew of a simple system that could improve the way people do business. A system that could be completely expressed in one short book that not only could be read quickly, but could benefit the reader for their entire business career. Plus, I was hoping I would never have to see another elevator speech competition. I still sometimes wake up in the middle of the night screaming. Ok, I'm joking about that, but you get my point.

A week later, I sat down in front of my computer,

opened up a new word processing document and typed, "Why did I write this book?"

Now you know why I wrote this book, but why should you care?

This book contains a simple four step system that can turn you into a networking master. You will be able to increase the number of people you excite about your company or products leading to more sales, improved suppliers relations, and increased word of mouth referrals. Successful people all over the world know that networking is one of the most effective ways to grow your business or promote your career. Learning to network more effectively is a fantastic use of your time. By creating your own personal Anti-Elevator Speech, you will be well on your way to gaining the success, prestige, and money you desire.

Chapter Two
The Concept

The first thing I need you to understand is the concept of the Anti-Elevator Speech. In theory, it is exactly the same concept as the elevator speech. You meet someone at a party, or a business event, or ... in an elevator ... and you want to share with them what you do. After all, every person you ever meet is a potential business contact, right? The difference is that the Anti-Elevator speech actually works in this setting. The standard elevator speech doesn't.

Too often I have heard a formal pitch speech referred to as an elevator speech. You do need a formal pitch presentation in your sales and or marketing arsenal, but a formal pitch is used in a completely different setting. A formal pitch is used when the person, or persons, you are talking to asked for said pitch and they are expecting exactly that. You already have their interest and this is an arranged meeting, for instance if you are going to their office. For this pitch you need about three minutes of scripted material worked out that quickly gives the details of your company or your proposal. Therefore, the Anti-Elevator Speech doesn't completely get rid of the elevator speech, it just changes the way you use it and when you use it. For instance, you should never use an elevator speech in an elevator.

There is no way that anyone can give an accurate account of what you do and how it could help someone else's business in the thirty seconds that you are on an elevator. It's absurd to think you can. The idea is not to fill their heads with every detail of your business in thirty seconds, but to generated enough interest to get that person excited enough to talk to you more when the elevator doors open. I know in my own experience, I have had my anti-elevator speech lead to lunch the same day, sometimes straight from the elevator to the restaurant.

The big problem with the elevator speech, is that I have heard it referred to as the elevator "pitch." Nobody wants to be pitched to in an elevator, or at a donut shop, or even at a network event. Don't you just hate it when you're eating dinner, the phone rings, you interrupt your meal to answer the phone and hear, "Good day madam, I would like to talk to you about your long distance phone services ..." CLICK! Am I right? That is a "pitch." At best they are annoying and worst they are down right out maddening. The government has passed laws to try and limit pitch phone calls. Why would you want to pick up where the phone company left off. Never pitch your company on an elevator or anywhere else on a first meeting.

WHAT!?! Yeah, you heard me, never pitch someone you've just met. I know this contradicts conventional wisdom and takes issue with a lot of books, magazine articles, consultants, and speakers, but I figure that if you were getting the results you wanted, you wouldn't be reading this book in the first place. Am I right? If you're reading a book with a name like the "Anti-Elevator Speech," you're probably looking to shake things up a bit. The same-old-same-old is just not going to cut it. If you wanted a book that was only going to support the way you're already thinking, you've come to the wrong place. So, you heard me right, NEVER pitch someone you've just met, period, end of story, turn off the oven it's done.

If you ask any great business person the one secret to their success, they will tell you it's relationships. It's not what you know, it's who you know. It's not who you know, it's how well you know them. The long and the short of it is people do business with people they like. You've heard the old adage, "it takes ten no's to get a yes." That percentage goes way up if you ask people who already know you and like you.

This is the main difference with the Anti-Elevator Speech, it's not a pitch, it's a conversation. You remember those, conversations? Those things you had with people you liked before you became an A-Type personality, pushing all the time, overworked, stressed out business person. Remember? For some of you this may have been a while ago, but think back. Conversations felt good didn't they? People talked to you, you talked to them, and the subjects flowed anywhere they wanted to go. Conversations are how you build relationships. That's the beauty of the Anti-Elevator Speech, it feels good. You're not pushing for a sale, so you're not stressed out and the person you're talking to doesn't feel pitched to so they're not stressed out either. Do you remember that AT&T slogan from the 90's, "reach out and touch someone?" Note that the slogan wasn't "reach out and PUNCH somebody in the face." A pitch, especially an unwelcomed pitch, can seem like a punch in the face. The Anti-Elevator Speech is an kinder, gentler and more effect way to reach out and touch someone. In fact, from this point on I'm not going to refer to the Anti-Elevator Speech as a speech at all. I'm going to call it the Anti-Elevator Conversation.

The pitch, or lack there of, is the difference in the concept between the elevator speech and the Anti-Elevator Conversation. Using the elevator speech you're trying to sell something. With the Anti-Elevator Conversation you're attempting to establish a relationship. My whole goal is to get to the point where the person I'm talking to will remember me fondly at our next encounter. I just love a, "hey Cliff, how have you been..." People who feel that way about you will want to do business with you, or at least show you pictures of their grand kids. I'll take this situation over a sales lead any day. You have a much better chance of doing business with a friend than a sales lead.

The fact that the Anti-Elevator Conversation is a conversation is exactly why I would never compete in an elevator speech competition. In the elevator speech competition, the competitors talk "AT" the master of ceremonies for three minutes. Who wants to be talked "AT" for three minutes? People want to be talked "WITH." In order for the Anti-Elevator Conversation to work, the master of ceremonies would have to talk back, which they don't do. Therefore, even if I wanted to be in an elevator speech competition, I'm sure I would lose. In fact, I would probably come in dead last. However, I would never be so happy about losing. I wouldn't want to be the winner at something that produced sales leads. Producing relationships, well that's a different story. You're a winner when you create relationships and by the end of this book I hope you'll agree with me.

Chapter #3
Two Seconds of Stunned Silence

I just spent the last half hour of my life trying to find out who first said, "if you can achieve two seconds of stunned silence, you can take over any conversation." I'm not sure who this genius was, but if I ever find out I'm going to edit this chapter to give him/her credit, they deserve it. Whoever this person was, they were brilliant and were the inspiration for step one in creating your Anti-Elevator Speech Conversation.

The first part of your Anti-Elevator Conversation is the Confusion Hook. It is a one sentence or less comment that will create two seconds of stunned silence from your conversational partner. This phrase will come right after they ask, "so what do you do?" This comment needs to be short, sweet, and confusing to the point of being profound. I know this step will need a lot more clarification, but for now just start thinking about what your company does and how you can sum up your business in one quick sentence.

At this point I want to discuss why you want a Confusion Hook. A typical elevator speech often begins with something like this:

"So, what do you do?"

"I'm a financial planner. I represent a number of large financial firms supplying insurance, 401k plans, retirement investments ..."

Unfortunately, what the person hears is:

"I'm a financial planner wah, wah, wah, wah, wah ..."

And what they are thinking is:

"Please Lord let this elevator stop. I don't even care if it's not my floor, I'm getting off. Help, help, I'm trapped!"

Obviously, this is not what you intended. The elevator speech doesn't work because the listener has nothing invested in this conversation. That is because it's not a conversation at all, it's a pitch. You are talking AT them and not WITH them. Once your listener invests in the conversation, you are well on your way to making a relationship. The Confusion Hook is how you get people invested in the conversation.

The quickest way to demonstrate this is with an example. I ran a successful company for years that I promoted with this quick phrase.

"So, what do you do?"

"You dream it up. We make it happen."

Ok, ok, ok, I know that's two quick sentences, but it's still short. Short is the real key, not how many sentences you have in your hook. The sentence, "we are a subsiderary for a large international pharmaceutical company that supplies hypertension medications to doctors and hospitals throughout the Mid-west," doesn't fall under the category of short. It is one sentence, but it isn't short. If you are saying more than ten words, it's too long. My statement above was eight words, so I'm good to go even though it's two sentences.

Here is how and why the above example works. When you read, "you dream it up, we make it happen," were you thinking, "WHAT?" That is exactly what I wanted you to think. That "what," that two seconds of confusion, that two seconds of stunned silence, gets the listener involved and invested in your conversation. This is the most important step in creating your Anti-Elevator Conversation and needs some serious thought and consideration. If this one short statement is compelling enough, it will create more networking opportunities for you than a boat load of elevator speeches. I'm not talking about getting business cards, but making true connections. The type of connections that lead to business relationships. The type of connections that will make people want to do business with you.

Now, comes the big asterisk, the big warning, after you have delivered your confusion hook, STOP TALKING! In conversations, many people make the mistake of filling the air with noise. Useless words that have little meaning and even less point. The greatest moment in any conversation or speech is the silence into which thoughts flow. If someone is always focusing on your words, they never have time to think about what you've just said. My wife, Marilyn, a business and personal relationships expert often says, "Don't just do something, stand there." I love this quote. This is what I want you to do after you deliver your Confusion Hook. Don't say a word, just stand there. Be quiet until they break the silence. As human beings we have been so trained to hate silence, that at first this may seem awkward and uncomfortable. Do it anyway. Without this step of silence, your Confusion Hook is worthless.

In a perfect Anti-Elevator Conversation opening, the next statement to be uttered by our contact should be, "so how exactly do you do that?" As soon as you hear those sweet, musical words, you have them invested in your conversation. There will be no wah-wah-wah in this conversation from that point on. The listener has invested a second question and their confusion in your conversation. Like any investment, people want to generate returns on their investments. The returns they want from the investment of their confusion, is to have their curiosity quenched and they won't be satisfied until it is. And that's where you come in. You will satisfy their curiosity by telling them what you do and how you do it.

However, if they don't reply with a question but instead say something like, "that's nice," then there is no reason to continue the conversation further. Time is precious, don't waste it. They are obviously not interested in what you have to say. Let's face it, most of the time when someone asks, "so what do you do," they really don't want to know. They are just making idle chitchat or trying to be polite because you have already asked them what they do and listened patiently as they bored you to tears with their three minute elevator speech. Their question only fills the air with noise, to remove the uncomfortable feeling people get from silence. Some people are so focused on themselves that they really don't want to know what you do, how you do it, or whom you do it to. Think of all the time you'll save not talking to these people. This is actually one of my favorite parts about the Anti-Elevator Conversation. I can quickly figure who is worth talking to. It's sort of like they have, "don't talk to me," stamped on their forehead. Like everyone else, I like to do business with people I like and have a relationship with. Someone who fails the confusion hook test does not want a relationship, they want your money. Trust me, you don't want to do business with a company like that.

Getting an, "I don't care" response, is actually a good thing. Don't get upset, that person just did you a favor. If you're at a networking event, your time there is valuable, no need to waste it with someone who isn't interested in what you have to offer. Just be polite and move along. Good response or bad, either way you are ahead of the game after the confusion hook.

Your confusion hook needs to be carefully thought out, scripted, memorized and made such a part of you that you can spit it out with comfort and ease at the drop of a hat. It should never sound forced or pitchy, just an off the cuff statement of fact. Let's analyze the details of my confusion hook from earlier.

My confusion hook, "you dream it up, we make it happen," was referring to Antler Software Technologies, a customized software house that created software to order based on the customer's specifications. Now imagine if my first statement was, "I run a customized software house that creates software to order based on your specifications." I hear the wah-wah-wahs playing in the distance already. What did my company really do? We listened to the needs and desires of our clients and created software to fill those needs. In short, you dream it up, we make it happen.

This is what I refer to as boiling down what you do into one quick phrase. If you can't do this for yourself or your company, then you haven't thought about what you do long enough. What is it you really do? Forget about your mission statement, your advertising, or your company motto, what do you really do? You may find that this will not only help you create your confusion hook, but may even help you focus on what's truly important in your business.

In my current company we supply presentation training to executives, lawyers, politicians, and educators to empower them to achieve the highest level of performance so they not only inform, but entertain their audiences. We also supply national caliber, hired gun speakers for events, workshops, sales presentations, and fund raisers. WOW! Now there is a mouthful. No one is going to listen to all of that, at least not right away. So, what do we do, "We Excite Audiences." I have boiled down what we do into three words. Short, sweet, and to the point or better yet, to the confusion.

"So what do you do?"

"We excite audiences."

{Two seconds of stunned silence. Don't just do something, stand there.}

"So ... how do you do that?"

I can't tell you how many times I have repeated this exact sequence at parties, business meetings, and networking events. It works like a charm almost every time and it can for you just as easily.

> You're a financial planner - "we give you a secure feeling."

> You're a custom home builder - "we create the American dream" or how about "we build dreams."

> You're a sport car salesperson - "I make you feel more alive."

Are you starting to get it yet? My guess is your wheels are already turning. In the three examples above, notice some of the key words used such as secure, dream, and alive. These words are feeling or action words. In my two confusion phases, I used the words dream and excite. These are really good words to put into your confusion hook because it makes people want to know more. When the car sales person says, "I make you feel more alive." Who doesn't want to feel more alive? This is the thought process that goes on in the listeners head leading them to ask the question, "how do you do that?"

Lets look at a few examples of such words that you may want to use in your confusion hook.

Feeling words or phrases:

Happy, jubilant, safe, powerful, excited, fun, joyful, delightful, warm feeling, relaxed, stress free, energized, etc.

Action words or phrases:

Exciting, focused, riveted, spell binding, effective, expressive, motivating, moving, absorbing, etc.

State of mind words:

Dreams, hopes, happiness, joy, pride, stressed, pressured, etc.

These are all great words to use in your confusion hook. These words reside in the part of the brain that invokes emotions and thoughts. This further enhances the power and effectiveness of your Anti-Elevator Conversation by getting people to think or feel. I have read many sales books that imply you don't want your customer to think, you want to do the thinking for both of you. Once again, I will have to buck the trend. I want my contacts to think as much as possible and to feel emotions even more. Emotions are powerful and will engage your contacts in a way that no other method can.

Structuring your confusion hook this way also has the benefit of setting up the mood of the conversation. Where does your confusion hook leave the listener? In a happy place? In a hopeful place? In a concerned place? Where do you want the conversation to go. Remember, if you can get two seconds of stunned silence, you take over any conversation. Never take over anything unless you're ready to lead. In this case you want to lead your listener into a productive, beneficial, and enlightening conversation for both of you.

It's easy to mess up the confusion hook with what you think you do. I did not create the next example so I can't take credit for it. I have read and/or heard many authors and speakers use this example, so I can't tell you who thought it up first. However, I have never heard a better example that more clearly demonstrates my point. Here is the statement, "if you are a drill bit salesperson, you don't sell drill bits, you sell holes." If you have never read or heard this before, please take the time to contemplate this statement. If you have read this before, take the time to carefully contemplate this important message again.

If a customer is buying drill bits, they have a need. That need is to create a round hole in something. They don't care about your drill, they care about the hole. The hole has to be drilled accurately, cheaply, and quickly. If this can be better achieved by a laser, they won't need your drill bits anymore. If you are a drill bit salesperson and you talk all about your drills, you probably won't get the sale. If you talk about their holes, you might just get that commission.

It's the same thinking that goes into a confusion hook. What is the end result of your product or service? You don't sell copy machines, you increase productivity. You don't supply flowers for weddings, you make a special day more special. Your confusion hook should never contain any element of how you do what you do, it should focus on the results.

"So what do you do?"

"We Excite Audiences."

That's what my company does. Whether we write the speech, coach on how to deliver the speech, or deliver the speech for you, our number one goal is to excite whatever audience our customers have. That's what our customers want, they want excited audiences.

I was recently speaking with a branch manager of a bank. Her bank had no fees for checking, money transfers, etc. That was their big selling point. She was trying to figure out her confusion hook. At first she didn't quite get it. She kept wanting to start with a statement like, "My bank..." or "I work for a bank." Right at that point I would stop her, and make her try again. After about three tries her eyes widened and I saw the light bulb go off as she said, "I save people money." Bingo! Who doesn't want to save money. It's a difficult task to get people to switch from their familiar and comfortable bank. If she uses the word bank in her confusion hook the contact will zone out. It was important for her to engage the listener before she mentioned how she saves them money.

Now, it's your turn. Think about your confusion hook by filling in the blank.

"So what do you do?"

Step 1 - "_____"

Step 2 - Don't just do something, stand there.

Chapter #4
The Reel

Your confusion hook has been delivered and you have achieved your two seconds of stunned silence. Where do you go from here? Your next two sentences, although not as important as the confusion hook, are trickier to construct. You have their attention, but the flames of their attention span won't last long unless you fuel the fire. Basically, all you've accomplished with the confusion hook is buying yourself two or three more sentences of focused attention. If the next couple statements in your conversation doesn't engage your listener, it's back to wah-wah-wah land.

Now it's time to clarify what you do, but not completely. You want to give them just enough information to get them interested enough to prompt you for more. So, let's review our conversation so far.

"So what do you do?"

"We excite audiences."

"How do you do that?"

"We're hired gun speakers and presentation consultants." {STOP TALKING!}

"What is a hired gun speaker?"

After the confusion hook, the next couple of sentences are used to reel them in. Once you can achieve that third question from the listener, you are set up for a good and productive conversation. A conversation that could easily lead to a relationship.

In the example above, I only used one sentence. It's not so important how many sentences you use, but how much more of the puzzle to give away. The reel can be much longer than your confusion hook, but not too long. A fifteen seconds reel is about the most you would want to use. Use your time effectively. Don't fill the air with pointless words. Lets consider the next bad example.

"We are a group of national class speakers that have been studying our craft for years. We speak on a number of different subjects from customer service, to presentation analysis methods. We can go into an auditorium and no matter what size the audience is we can light them up and get them on their feet for a standing ovation. We also offer a wide variety of presentation training services from keynotes to workshops for corporations, associations, and individuals including executives, lawyers, and politicians."

Z-Z-Z-z-z-z-z ... Shoot, I just put myself to sleep and it's my company. Less is more. Just because you have fifteen seconds, doesn't mean you have to use it all. I'm sure you have lots of valuable information to share and you'll get your chance once you have the listener's attention and they have invested themselves in your conversation by asking that third question. Wait to be prompted for more.

Once again, if you get a response like, "oh, that's nice," do yourself and your listener a favor by shutting up. They're just not interested, let it go and get on with your life. If you got back all the time you spent boring people to death who are clearly not interested, imagine how productive you would have been. Save yourself the time and spare them the agony of listening to your pitch if they're not interested.

In the words of Gene Simons, bass player with the legendary rock band KISS, "you get rich by getting 10% of the people to love you, not everyone to like you." Or, to paraphrase Abraham Lincoln, you can't interest all the people all the time. Pushy people get a reputation and not a good one. Don't push, wait for them to come to you.

Just like after the confusion hook, you need to stop talking after the reel. Let there be some dead air in order to give your contact the time to ask that third question.

Lets look at a few examples:

Sports car salesperson:

> **Hook** - "I make you feel more alive."

> **Reel** - "By giving you the ride of your life."

Caterer:

> **Hook** - "I send your mouth to heaven."

> **Reel** - "With food that will drive you and your

guests wild."

Marketer:

Hook - "I make your business boom."

Reel - "By cementing your brand into the minds of your buyers."

Notice that in each case, the reel didn't give away all the details. Notice that the car salesperson didn't say, "I sell Ford Mustangs." The caterer didn't add, "I supply all your catering needs for your next event." The marketer didn't continue with, "we create television commercials." If they had coughed up too many details in the reel, they would have shut down the conversation by making their contact jump to conclusions about what they do. We don't want your contact to think, "oh yuck, car salesperson. I don't want a car. I'd better get out of here."

When thinking about your reel, you should decide on something that allows for multiple answers. The caterer above said, "with food that will drive you and your guests wild." That could be a number of things. They may run a restaurant or perhaps they sell frozen food. A number of different kinds of companies could have that same reel. This is what I mean by not giving away all the details.

The marketers comment of, "by cementing your brand into the minds of your buyers," could refer to just about anything from magazines to business seminars. It's this open ended statement that continues the confusion state.

The reel is where you can start to talk about how you deliver the results, but be careful not to give it all away. You want just enough information to continue the confusion a bit little longer.

Now it's your turn.

"So what do you do?"

Step 1- Confusion Hook

" _____ "

Step 2 - Don't just do something, stand there

"And exactly how do you do that?"

Step 3 - The Reel

" _____ "

" _____ "

Step 4 - Don't just do something, stand there

Chapter #5
And Then?

And then nothing. That's it, the conversation has started. You have quickly guided the listener to a series of conversational paths they can choose. At this point they are more in control of the conversation than you are. They will decide which path the conversation should take. All you need to do is follow where they lead.

So how simple was that? All you needed to create and memorize was your Confusion hook and your Reel. This was a total of five sentences at most and short sentences at that. Pretty much anyone can apply this system. Therefore, not only is the Anti-Elevator Conversation more effective than an elevator speech, it's easier to implement.

What happens next is the art of conversation. Knowing how to talk so people will want to hear what you have to say is a skill in itself. Although the art of conversation could be a book all on it's own, lets look at some of the ways to follow the path your listener wants to take. These are key points in the conversational arts that will help with the follow up to the Anti-Elevator Conversation in a way that is productive and meaningful.

The first and most important aspect of the post Anti-Elevator Conversation starter is to listen way more than you talk. Don't talk at someone, talk with them. World class conversationalists will only talk about a third of the time in a conversation. In a networking situations this is important. There is no way you can understand the needs of the listener if you are doing all the talking. Your contact doesn't care about how you do things, how much profit you make, or the name of your founder, they care about what they need. Pay attention to their needs and a relationship is bound to follow.

It's important to understand that there are two different types of talking I'm referring to when I say don't talk so much. The first type of talking is the sounds you make with your mouth. The second type of talking is the sub-conversation you have in your mind. I call this mind speak. Have you ever noticed it is difficult to carry on two conversations at once? It's amazing how many people carry on two conversations all the time. One conversation is with the person they are talking to and the other conversation is with themselves.

Many people are so busy thinking about the next clever and witty comment they are going to make, that they're not really listening to their partner at all. The term great conversationalist is sort of a misnomer to me, for it implies that you are talking. The most important part of a conversation is the time you spend listening. I mean really focusing on someone. Few people really focus on their conversational partners. Oh sure they nod their head and sort of grunt now and then, but to truly listen will make you someone worth listening to in return. When you truly listen to someone, you will pick up the nuances of what they really want to talk about. When it is your turn to talk, speak slow, deliberate and with purpose. When you're not talking, shut your mind down and focus on their words. Don't think about your next sentence or what you plan to order for lunch. Look them straight in the eye and listen. Now that you are thinking about this concept on a conscious level, you may find that there is an entirely different plane of conversations that you have never experienced before. People who I have shared this concept with, often have interesting revelations after they have tried it out. Sometimes they find that people talk way too much without saying anything. Other times they come to the realization that they talk way too much without saying anything. Try this out for yourself and see how it feels. Just remember, don't mind speak while the other person is talking.

This is the way someone who uses the Anti-Elevator Conversation differentiates themselves from someone giving an elevator pitch. People who are giving a sales pitch are rarely listening to you. They have a game plan that doesn't include you. I remember when my family was looking to purchase new windows for our home. A salesman showed up at our door. Very early on in my conversation with him, I shared that I hated high pressure sales and didn't like to make decisions on the spot. It couldn't have been more than two minutes after I made that comment, that he went into this twenty minute, high pressure, you have to decide right now to get this price sales pitch. He didn't get the sale. This salesman made the classic mistake of not listening. If he had, he would have changed his tactics to better accommodate my preferences. He also talked at me and not with me which, as you may have guessed, I hate that too.

The next salesman came into my home, gave me a

broucher of the windows he sold, measured my windows, asked if I had any questions (which I did), and then quietly left promising to get a quote to me in a couple of days (which he did). I don't know if he was reading my body language or if that was just his selling style, but it was certainly my buying style. In a week he was installing new windows for me.

Matching the vibrational energy of your patners can really help.

Learning to Read Your Partner

Another technique used by great conversationalists, can be achieved by watching facial gestures. Even when people are not saying anything, they are often communicating their desires and interests. There are many differnet techniques to do this, but in this chapter we are only going to discuss three different skills. Whereas, this does not seem like a lot, mastering this three technique will put you way ahead of the game. The three different skills are; the agreement, thinking mode, and the surprise.

The Agreement

The most common non-verbal cue people share is the head nod. People instinctively nod their heads up and down in a "yes, I agree" manner when they agree with what you are saying or they find it interesting. This gesture can be quite small at times, so you need to keep an eye open for it. The slightest movement of the head is enough to let you know that you are striking a chord with your listener.

Few businesses today offer only one service or product. To survive in a tough competitive environment, companies have to diversify. By noticing head nods, you can avoid talking about products, services, or concepts in which the listener has no interest. When you get that first head nod, steer the conversation to the details of the topic you were discussing when the head nod occurred. The more head nods you can get in a conversation the better you are doing.

Let me share an example. Let's say you are a business consultant. You quickly talk about your business plan creation services - nope, no head nod. They must already have one of those. You quickly discuss your employee benefits planning services - nope, no head nod. Maybe they don't make the decisions about that service. You mention your international business marketing wing, and there goes the head. Your company may supply ten other product lines as well, but who cares, you have struck a chord. At this point you may want to follow up with a question to determine the extent of their interest like, "do you have a need for international marketing?" The funny thing about using this technique, is that after a while people will start to think you're psychic. You'll always seem to know what they want to talk about.

Thinking Mode

Another technique of facial expression reading, is to notice eye movement. If your listener looks up to the left (note, that is to your right, but their left), or down to the left, they have entered thinking mode.

It is important to note that this is only true if they enter REM mode. REM stands for "Rapid Eye Movement" and is most commonly associated with sleeping/dreaming. Years ago, psychologists noticed that if a sleepers eyes were moving back and forth, then they were dreaming. This connection between eye movement and thinking can also be noticed when someone is awake. Just looking down to the left doesn't mean you are thinking unless you start REM. Just looking down could mean that you are really bored. Looking up to the left without REM could mean there is something interesting on the ceiling. Therefore, when they look off to the left, the next thing you need to look for is REM. Their eyes will start dancing back and forth. If you see this, then the following techniques apply.

Once your conversational partner goes into "Thinking Mode," their focus on what you are saying has diminished. They have entered the realm of mind speak. They are basically having a second conversation with themselves. This is probably not the best time to say something profound or significant. They could be thinking about something useful to you. Perhaps they are thinking about how they can use your services or about someone they know who would be interested in what you have to say. Or, they could also be thinking about what they want to order for lunch. It's hard to tell sometimes if you have struck a chord or lost them all together. Either way, noticing this eye movement is a powerful tool in creating productive conversations.

People who talk too much, often step on the other person's thought processes. Once someone looks down and begins to think, let them think. Keep talking, but keep the conversation light. When they look back at you, they have formulated their thoughts. This is the perfect time to let them talk. If you keep talking after they look back, you could squash an important insight, idea, or comment. By the time you quit talking, they may have forgotten what they were thinking about. I'm sure you've heard people say, "I had something important to tell you, but I've completely lost it." If this has ever happened to you, it is probably because you have stepped on their thought process. To capture or enhance their thought process, when they look back up ask them a "Pass The Torch Question."

A pass the torch question is when you are making it clear that you want them to talk. Questions such as:

"So what do you think?"

"How do you feel about that?"

"Share your thinking about this with me." (I know, not a question, but it still counts)

"Do you have any additional ideas?"

These examples all make it clear to your contact that you're planning to shut up now and let them talk. If these questions are placed strategically at the moment they reestablish their eye contact, you will often get to hear what they were just thinking about. Not only does this improve the quality of the conversation by nurturing the thought process, but it will make the other person feel like they have been heard and understood.

Unless of course, what they were thinking about was

what to have for lunch. In this case they will just seem lost when you ask your pass the torch question. However, this is still a good thing, because the question will refocus them on your conversation and less on lunch. Never make a point of their loss of focus. A comment like, "it seems like I lost you there," will just embarrass them. Just give them a few seconds to rejoin the discussion and let them lead the next section of the conversation.

You can further subdivide the thinking process into two sub-categories. The first one is looking down to the left. This means they are scanning their minds for memories. They are looking for items in their experience that relate to what you are saying. Or perhaps, they're trying to remember what their spouse asked them to pick up at the store on the way home. If they were thinking about your conversation, they may be searching for a contact name or a specific application for your services. Sometimes we can go fishing for their thoughts by modifying our pass the torch question like the examples below.

> "Is there anything in your experience that relates to this?"

> "When have you needed a product like this before?"

> "Do you know someone who could benefit from what I offer?"

Note that in all three of these cases, we are referring to items with which they have had experience. By wording the question in this way, we may further draw out the thoughts of the listener. Note phrases like, "in your experience," and "when have you needed," both refer to things that they already have in their minds. It is not calling for the creation of new ideas.

In the second case, when they are looking up and to the left, they are formulating new ideas or concepts. Something you have said is making them think. This can be a good thing. They are about to add a new element to the conversation that could allow you to connect on a deeper level. In this case, you want to ask your pass the touch question in a way that promotes new thoughts.

"Do you have any additional thoughts on this?"

"How could this help you in the future?"

"What's your thinking on this subject?"

These are all questions that promote new ideas. This takes practice. Don't expect to be good at this technique right away. In the beginning, you might just want to notice their loss of eye contact and not add the pass the torch questions until you are skilled at recognizing the timing of such events. In time you will become skilled at using this conversational technique and apply it almost by instinct. This will allow you to create a more positive and beneficial result from all your personal and business conversations.

The Surprise

The last facial gesture we will talk about is the eyebrow raise. A slight raise of one or both eyebrows indicates an element of surprise. Something you have said made them look at things in a new way or caught them off guard. This gesture is often accompanied by a head nod, but is quite different than the head nod alone. If you make a comment like, "our product will cut your drying time by two thirds," and right there you see the eyebrow raise. That's it. This is a key point they want to know more about. There are two things you can do at this point. The first one is to start giving additional details on this subject. The second is to inject an interest question such as, "does that sound good to you?" Whereas both of these techniques are good, I prefer the question approach. Remember my motto, listen more than you talk. The question, "does that sound good to you," can help you gage just how much interest they have. If they respond with, "yes, we have a real need for that," you are half way to a sale. If they comment, "perhaps, I'm really not sure," this means you should move along with the conversation, but make a mental note to bring this subject up again in a follow up meeting, phone call, email or even later in the same conversation.

By combining the concepts of focused listening, listening more than you talk, and reading facial gestures you will be well on the way to being a master conversationalist.

Chapter #6
It's All In The Cards

How to deal with business cards can be a tricky business. If you don't think business cards and how to use them is an important topic, you are probably not using your business cards as effectively as you could. Lets take a look at some important aspects of business cards.

I realize that business cards are pretty cheap in the scheme of things, but handing them out to anyone with a pulse is one of the biggest mistakes you can make. In one of my favorite scenes from the movie, "Willy Wonka and the Chocolate Factory," starring Johnny Dep as Willy Wonka, one of the adults taking a tour of Willy's chocolate factory hands Willy his business card in an effort to sell nuts for Willy's candy bars. As soon as the card giver looks away, Willy flings the card over his shoulder in disgust. It's a funny scene in the movie, but not so funny in real life. Nobody likes to have business cards thrust in their face. If they want your card, they will ask for it. In the process of asking you for your card, they will take note of the card and it will mean a lot more to them later when they empty their pockets or find your card floating at the bottom of their purse.

This holds doubly true for flyers and other informational materials. If you push your flyer into the face of everyone you meet right in the beginning of your conversation, you have probably only contributed another piece of paper to a garbage land fill somewhere. People hate this, don't do it. If they ask, "do you have any information on this," now you give them your flyer. Not only is this more effective, but you save a little money on printing too. How often have you returned from an industry show only to empty your carrying bag and throw out three quarters of product handouts without giving them a second look?

Another tricky part of the business card swap, is what to do when someone gives you their business card. In many Asian cultures, they have developed a ritual around handing out business cards. They present the card holding it with both hands in the upper corners of the card. The card is presented facing you so you can read it immediately. The receiver of the card then takes it by the bottom corners with two hands, studies it, acknowledges the reception of the card and then carefully puts the card safely away while the giver observes. The receiver never writes on the card either. Asians believe that business cards are an extension of the giver and writing on it would be like writing on the giver's forehead. It just not done.

Whereas this seems like a bit of overkill to many western cultures, especially Americans, I believe there are many parts of the Asian ritual that have a lot of merit. The honoring of someone else's business card, is like honoring their business or them. Grabbing their card and nonchalantly throwing it in your pocket, conveys the message that you really don't care about the card, them, or their business and you will probably just throw it away when you get back to the office. Ouch, that hurts, right? No one wants to feel like they were just dismissed. Take the time to care about the person and their business card.

When you received someone's business card, take the time to really look at it. Comment on it and let the person see you put it away someplace secure like a card slot in your folder or a specialized card carrying case. I have found in many cases when I do this, and I was the one who asked for a business card first, they will ask for my card right after. By respecting their business card, they feel respected. People like doing business with people they respect and who respect them. At first glace the Asian idea that a business card is an extension of the giver may not land with you, but trust me the Asian people are on to something here. Taking a few extra seconds to honor someone's business card goes a long way in building relationships.

I have found that many people spend little or no time creating their business cards. I believe this is a huge mistake. Your business card is an extension of you. You want your card to not only have contact information, but portray you in a positive and memorable light. I want to briefly share with you some of the do's and don'ts I have noticed over of years of viewing thousands of business cards.

First off, be unique. How many cards have you seen that are white with black lettering. People who have business cards like this often say that they are "business-like." Business-like is really overrated. These cards are boring, predictable, and totally forgettable. You want your card to stand out from the crowd. As I'm writing this section, I'm scanning through a pile of about forty cards I received at a local business expo. Let's see which ones catch my eye.

Here is a black card with white lettering, you don't see that much. Here is a full color card. Of course it's from a graphics design shop so that makes sense. I remember that booth now, interesting graphics. Here is one that folds out. Maybe a bit of overkill, but the card does stand out. I loved the cards from a company called YOUniqueCards.com. I saw their booth at this expo and thought they were really on to something. This company was promoting their business card creation/printing service. They make personalized business cards based on a full color caricature of you. These drawings are similar to the ones you get at the state fair for $20 from a street vendor, except better painted and in full, vibrant color. These cards will make you stand out from the crowd. Cards this elaborate may not be your style, and that's fine, but being boring and forgettable is not a style, it's just bad business. Think about what you want your card to say about you and find a way to say it.

Are you in financial services? How about a big, gold money sign on your card. Are you a car salesperson? How about a picture of you driving one of those cars. Think creatively. Be unique.

As for me, my business card has a giant head shot of me with a playful grin on my face. If you have ever seen me speak live, that pretty much says it all. Above my head is our web-site name ExciteYourAudience.com in a curved set of letters that invokes power with a modern look. My card is totally unique and memorable.

I was at a business expo and a young, smartly dressed woman approached me and said, "hey, you're that big head guy." Now, I had to think about that for a few seconds, then I realized she meant my business card. At least that's what I told myself. Since then, I have begun joking about my card telling people it's the big head card. They laugh and it helps them remember me. One thing for sure, my card stands out in the crowd of boring cards. I've had some people comment that my card is silly, and that's great because is means they took notice of it.

My second tip is to include a comment on your card about what you do. I can't tell you how many cards I get that state the person's name, company name and a phone number. That's it. Often the company name on the card is something like Wilker and Wright. That doesn't tell me anything. If I look at this card two days later I won't have a clue who they are. If you meet forty people at a meeting, it's tough to remember everyone by name, at least for me. Put your tag line, business type, or something that will help me connect your face to the card. This will make me much more prone to give you a call. I receive a lot of business cards. I want to remember you, but I need you to give me a break, or a least a clue. A great thing to put on your business card is your Confusion Hook. That's what I have on mine. In fact, that is also my web-site address, ExciteYourAudience.com.

I have asked people who sport these non-identifiable cards why they do it. I have heard some lame answers like, "I do more than one thing," or "the card is cheaper that way." I don't know what business you're in, but when I get a new client that's worth some serious coin. Business cards are cheap, but that doesn't mean you should be. Spend a little bit more money on your business cards, they are a reflection of you. If you have more than one business venture, have more than one business card. I personally have four different business cards. A card that says, "Sue Sprite - Business Consultant and Master Gardener," is just going to confuse people. Make two different cards, one for your love of flowers and the other for your love of business.

Look out, I'm getting on my soapbox now. Here is my personal pet peeve. Stop using lettering that is so small it looks like it was written by Tibetan monks who paint complex art on a grain of rice. I'm not as young as I use to be and I can't read that type of lettering anymore without a microscope. It's annoying, knock it off. At the very least your name, phone number, and email address should be easy to read. Just because you have the eye sight of a falcon, doesn't mean the rest of us do.

And finally, don't use swirly, curly, cutesy lettering styles that are hard to read. If I can't tell a Q from an O or a L from a K it is going to make it hard or even embarrassing for me to call up your company and ask for, "I'm not sure if it's Kelly or Shelly and it looks like Michelputz." A nice clean lettering style is always the better choice.

Don't take your business cards or how you use them for granted. It's the people that take a little bit more time to work out the details that end up with the sales. Make your business card unique, clear, and readable. Give cards only to people who ask for them. Honor the card you are given. It is time to start a business card tradition of your own.

Chapter #7
Take Your Time

In a recent networking event I attended, a nicely dressed young man walked up to me and asked, "Do you have a website?" When I answered yes, he asked me for my card, told me he designed web-sites, would review my web-site and call me. With that he gave me his card and took off. He never asked anything about me or my company. I started thinking about that scene from the Willy Wonka movie again. Odds of him redesigning my web-site ... ZERO. There were two people talking with me, to whom he did the same thing, and the comments about him were not favorable. However, he did give me a better chance to connect with the two people I was talking to. Now all three of us had something in common. We were all annoyed with him. There are a lot of people who design web-sites, why would I use someone who just annoyed me, clearly didn't want to know me, and didn't take the time to care.

I'm about to part with conventional wisdom here. I know there are a lot of books, videos, and audio tapes that will disagree with me and that's fine. You may have even read some of these books. You may even disagree with me and that's fine too. I just want to you keep an open mind during this next section. Remember that if you were totally happy with the results you're getting, you wouldn't be reading this book at all, now would you?

The classic mistake made by many people at a networking event, is the idea that you have to meet everyone. You don't have time to spare. You have to keep moving. Shove your business card in their faces and move on. Heaven forbid you should miss somebody. The only thing you'll accomplish with this tactic is irritating everyone in the room. I would much rather have a meaningful conversation with ten people, than a meaningless conversation with a hundred. If you can walk out of a group networking opportunity with one new client, one new source for services or products, a small hand full of solid leads, or best of all a friend you may run into later, you've had a really good day. You can't judge the success of a networking opportunity by how many flyers you handed out. The true measure of networking success is how many people you can call a few days later that won't duck your call. You do this by taking the time to connect.

For those of you who didn't agree with me at first, think about how you felt the last time someone walked up to you, handed you their business card right off the bat and then walked away. Didn't introduce themselves, didn't ask your name, didn't even ask if you care about what they do just stuffed a card in your face. How did that feel? Most people just start looking around for a garbage can to pitch the card in.

Don't collect business cards, collect relationships. I know people who have amassed an impressive collection of business cards, but can't tell you a thing about any of the people who gave them the cards, not a single thing. To me this is a complete failure of the process. If all you're looking for is email addresses and phone numbers ... well ... you can get those out of the yellow pages. All you're doing is getting people to cold call and we all know how well cold calls work, right? I have found that the majority of my most promising leads are not with the person who gave me their card, but with someone the card holder knows. In my slowed down approach to networking, I have found that often my strongest leads don't appear until five to ten minutes into a conversation. I know what you're thinking, "how long do you want me to talk Cliff?" As long as it takes.

Most people in a networking environment are thinking about themselves. What is in it for them is foremost on their minds. That's why the idea of a networking event can be relatively goofy. You're trying to sell them, they are trying to sell you, it's like the clash of the titans or maybe Larry, Moe, and Curly. There is lots of noise being made, but little is really getting accomplished.

I was at a networking event just yesterday, about ten minutes into a conversation mainly about the other person's products, he pulled out someone else's business card, circled a small web-site address on the back of the card, and suggested that I contact them right away. This was a contact for twelve speaking gigs. Twelve gigs! That's more than a gig a minute. Sure, in ten minutes I could have met ten people using the traditional elevator speech approach, but the net results of those ten contacts would have probably been zero speaking gigs. So I didn't meet nine people, so what. I wasn't there to collect business cards. Collecting business cards isn't like collecting baseball cards. Baseball cards go up in value over time, business cards don't.

Relationships on the other hand, always go up in value over time. This is a universal truth understood by almost every successful person on the planet.

Slow down and get to know people. It's the best time you'll ever spend.

Chapter #8
It's Not About You

In my successful CD set on public speaking, "Audience in the Palm," I mention again and again how a good speech is not about you. The speech should always be about your audience. What's in it for them. As soon as a presenter forgets that, they have destroyed the effectiveness of their speech.

Networking is the same way. Networking is not about you, but about what you can do for everyone else. Don't make your first contact about the sale. Whereas you may get a couple of sales this way, you will not get any relationships. Relationships are more important in the long run. What would you rather have five people that each purchased one item from you, or one person that purchased five items from you? This is not a trick question. The answer is the one person. Not only will that one person probably buy more than five items from you eventually, they are way more likely to refer you to others. If someone buys one item it's a sale. If they buy five items over a period of time, they have become a fan.

Have you ever known a fan of a rock band? Maybe you are one. I'm not talking about someone who buys a CD here or there, I'm talking about a real fan. They buy CD's, go to all the concerts, buy t-shirts and programs, request songs to be played on the radio, and tell everyone they know about this wonderful band. That's a fan. Isn't that the kind of customers you want? Rock bands that generate this type of fan give everything they have, every night, to their audience. They don't have big egos, at least on stage, it's all about the audience. This applies to everyone you meet as well. Make it about them.

A great way to make it about them is to be the first one to ask, "so what do you do." I always jump in right away with that question. Then, I truly listen to the other person. I don't do the typical, wait, wait, wait until it's my turn to talk, I really listen. I focus on what they are saying and more than that, I look for ways to help them. I want you to really hear what I'm saying here. I look for ways to help them, not to help me. I don't focus on ways I can sell them stuff, I look for ways I can be of assistance. Perhaps I have a sales lead for them. Is there an organization I'm familiar with that can help solve a problem for them? Would one of my competitors be able to supply their needs?

I know what you're thinking. "WHAT!?! Cliff, did you really just say that? You want me to send a contact to a competitor? Are you nuts?"

I may be nuts, but not about this. If you truly listen and care about the person you are talking to, you may find instances where the products or services offered by one of your competitors better matches the needs of this contact. In this case, I highly recommend that you refer this person to that other source. Let's face it, if you don't have the exact service this person is looking for, they won't be happy with your products even if they decide to buy it. By referring them to another source, you show that you care more about them than making a fast buck. In the process you are actually improving your bottom line. A dissatisfied customer is never a good thing. I have always lived by the motto, "good news travels slowly, bad news travels like wild-fire." You don't want there to be any bad news about your company. Don't think about short term goals, think about long term relationships. Believe me, this contact may go buy from that other company, but when they have a need that the other company can't supply, they will be back.

Even if there is never an opportunity for you to refer someone to a competitor, the fact that you would, puts you in the correct state of mind. By deciding now that you would do this if the situation arose, you have decided to help your contact out at any cost. Isn't this the type of person you would want to do business with?

You have to care. That is the long and short of it. The best business people are the ones that care about their clients for more than just bolstering their profits. You should always be looking for a way to help everyone else. Whereas this may seem altruistic, and it is, the rewards of a steady stream of this type of behavior will be reaped by you for years to come. Whatever you put out into the universe echos back to you ten fold. If you put out an uncaring, I'm in it for myself attitude, what are you going to get back?

I know we live in a world that seems to promote the rat race attitude. Reality TV shows promote backstabbing, money grubbing, you have to lose for me to win approaches to life, but that's just television. In real life good guys often finish first. A perfect example of this is Bob Taylor, president of Taylor Guitars one of the largest acoustic guitar manufacturers in the United States. Bob treats his employees like family, shares innovations in guitar design freely, and even takes fishing trips with the presidents of competing companies. Bob cares. We all need to be a little bit more like Bob and less like the reality TV show of the week.

Do whatever it takes to help others and you will be remembered for it.

Chapter #9
Know When To Shut Up

Have you ever heard of the term over-selling? Basically, this term refers to the effect that happens if you keep promoting the virtues of the product after your customer has agreed to buy. You may just talk yourself out of a sale. This effect can also come to bear in a networking situation as well.

If you recall, I stated that you should never hand out your card unless someone asks for it. In a networking situation, a contact asking for your card is a victory. You've made them interested enough to want to call you at a later time. Be careful how long you engage the person after they have ask for your card. You could just end up talking yourself out of a business relationship.

This is especially true in a rich networking environment. The term rich networking environment refers to a location or event where there are many potential contacts to talk to. This can be a trade show, industry workshop, association meeting, or an event especially set up for networking. In such an environment, people don't want to spend too much time with one person. I know I stated that this is a mistake, and it is, but not everyone has read this book yet. Many people want to talk to as many contacts as possible. Taking up too much of their time will just irritate them.

Be sure to keep your eyes open for subtle clues that indicate your contact wants to end the discussion. Loss of eye contact is a dead give away. If the person starts looking at other people or other trade show booths, wrap the conversation up and move on.

If you're not sure, there are some test statements you can ask to gage your contact's continuing interest level in your conversation. A perfect statement is:

> "I'm sure you have many more people to meet. I don't want to tie up too much of your time, so I'd better let you go."

This statement demonstrates that you honor their time, but still hints that you wouldn't mind talking longer. At this point you can judge their reaction. A response like "it was nice meeting you," confirms that it's time to bring an end to this conversation. A comment more like, "wait, I would like to hear more," means you're really hitting a home run. Keep talking as long as they would like. The longer you talk the more you cement your relationship.

Chapter #10
How to wrap things up

If a conversation goes especially well, make sure to create a short action plan. It is important to note that you should only create an action plan if you plan to take action. Don't make promises you don't intend to keep. People don't mind you saying no, but they hate it when you say yes and then don't deliver. If the contact is interesting enough that you want to have further discussions, make plans to do so. If not, shut up and move on to the next person.

I'm sure you have heard women complain about men who say they will call for a date and they never do. It's not just women looking for romance who hate this. Everyone in any situation hates to be waiting for a call. Don't say you're going to call, email, or fax and then fail to do so. Not only is this not living your life with integrity, but you will get a bad name in your industry as someone that does not follow through.

Your follow up plan should be specific. If you're going to call, state what day and time you will call them. Not only will this make you look organized, but it will actually make you more organized. This type of follow up is uncommon, but it should be common. If the contact is busy at the time you suggest, you will save yourself the trouble of making the call. This works in reverse too. If they are calling you, set up a time. Emails are a bit looser, but even with emails you should let your contact know when they should expect your email. A comment like, "you can expect my email by the end of the week," is fine, but phone calls or office visits should be set up with an exact time.

Another good idea is to make specific notes about your contact. Even if you have a fantastic memory, it is quite possible to meet ten, fifteen, even twenty interesting people at an event. The next day when you review those business cards, it may become difficult to remember who said what, the follow up plan you created, or even why this person was interesting in the first place. Carry a folder, paper pad or a personal voice recorder and make a memo of each conversation that has piqued your interest. Be sure to include the person's name, email, phone number, and web address if appropriate. Also include any personal information you may have learned about this person and the follow up action that needs to be taken. A short paragraph is so much easier to remember than a few words scrawled on the back of a business card. If possible, do this in a place where your contact will not see or hear you, especially if you are using a voice recorder. Making contact notes in front of the person may make them feel like nothing more than a sales call. Remember we want relationships not sales leads.

Chapter #11
It Doesn't Work

I want to share with you why I decided to add this chapter to the 2nd edition of my book. After the book was published, I went on a speaking tour for the book which continues today. In fact, "The Anti-Elevator Speech - THE SPEECH," is one of my most popular seminars. During many question and answer periods, I often get asked a similar question to this one:

> "At a business networking meeting I was asked to stand up and talk about my company for 30 seconds. The Anti-Elevator Speech didn't work at all. How do I handle this situation?"

My inquisitive audience members are absolutely correct. The Anti-Elevator Speech was never designed to work in this setting, because you're the only one talking. You have no one to bounce your Anti-Elevator hook and reel off. This is not a conversation at all, it's more like a mini speech. There are a number of local and national networking groups that work exactly this way. These groups normally have formal meetings on a weekly or monthly basis. The format of these meeting is very structured. One by one, everyone stands up and introduces themselves, telling the group about their company. Many people feel thrust into the spotlight when this happens. That is why I refer to this situation as a "Spotlight Moment." The stress of a spotlight moment can cause people to make a critical mistake. They are so worried about what they are going to say when it's their turn, that they don't listen to what everyone else is saying. Thereby, they miss out on hearing bio's from people they probably should meet. This is a problem that needs to be addressed. If you are better prepared for your spotlight moment, you will be more present for the rest of the meeting.

When I get this question at my seminars, it would be easy enough for me to say, "I'm sorry the Anti-Elevator Speech isn't meant for that," and move on to the next question. Unfortunately, that would leave people hanging. They would have sat though an entire hour or two of listening to me yak, just to be disappointed. Maybe you feel the same way right now. Maybe you're thinking, "I read this whole dang book and I'm still going to blow it at my next network meeting."

I feel your pain. That's why I have added this chapter. I want to be there for you. OK, maybe I'm not ready to give the toast at your wedding or help you move your couch, but I want to be there with information you need to avoid the dreaded elevator speech in any situation. I haven't journeyed with you this long to see you drop back into bad habits. Even in this situation, elevator speeches stink. I guarantee that what you have learned so far will not be in vain.

During spotlight moments, the elevator speech is actually useful to you. "What ... did Cliff just say elevator speeches are useful?!? Is he losing his mind?!?" It's true, the elevator speech can be useful by contrast. Elevator speeches are exactly what everyone else in the room will be doing. One person after another will stand up and bore everyone to tears with their elevator speeches. This is the perfect time for you to blow everyone's mind with a new approach. By being different, you will stand out in the crowd, and that is exactly what you want. Their dull elevator speeches will make you shine in contrast. So, everyone else's elevator speeches are useful because they will make you look more interesting. Let a few elevator speeches numb people into a catatonic coma and you'll be the star of the show in comparison.

In marketing there is an old adage, "look at what everyone else is doing and do something else." Next time you're at a formal networking group, watch what everyone else is doing and do something else. "What else?" I'm glad you asked. In the pages that follow, I will give you a number of possibilities to peak the interest of the crowd. Some may not be right for you, and that's OK. Use the one that fits your personality, your company's objectives, or just feels right at the time. However, I want to challenge you to try the uncomfortable ones and see if you can pull them off. Sometimes the best way to learn how to swim is to be dumped into the deep end of the pool. When you feel uncomfortable, it's probably because you're growing. Don't be afraid to fail, it will make you stronger in the long haul.

Possibility #1: Revamping Your Anti-Elevator Conversation

If you structure your Anti-Elevator hook and reel correctly, you can use them for your spotlight moments. To accomplish this, use a professional speaking technique called "mind questions." Polished professional speakers will use mind questions to grab an audience. This technique gives the impression that the speaker is reading the audiences' mind. When the speaker connects in this way, the audiences tunes in. Mind questions are a simple technique in theory, but can take a life-time to perfect. Fortunately, you will only have to perfect two statements, your hook and your reel. That shouldn't take too long to learn if you apply the tips below.

For a mind question to work, speakers ask a question that at least 80% for their audience will answer in the same way. The audience is not suppose to answer out loud, the speakers just wants them to see the answer in their minds. It is not a coincidence that an 80% positive response is also what you'd expect from a good hook. Both of these conversation techniques are built on the same psychological theory. The difference is that a mind question works on a group. Another difference is that a hook either works or it doesn't. A mind question can work on everyone eventually. Stragglers who don't initially response in the desired manner, often change their minds when they see everyone else agreeing with you. This takes advantage of the mob mentality. Everyone wants to belong to the group.

Like the hook, your should allow at least two seconds of silence afterward for the crowd to answer the question in their minds. Then, restate the obvious answer. This description can be a bit confusing, so let me clear things up with an example:

"Do you want to make more money?" (Two seconds of silence) "Of course you do, who doesn't?"

The only real difference between mind questions and Anti-Elevator hooks, is that you give the response instead of your partner. Other than that, the two techniques are exactly the same.

Let's look at an actual Anti-Elevator Conversation and how it can be converted. I'll use mine, as it was discussed in chapter two. As a reminder, here is my Anti-Elevator Conversation.

> **Conversation Partner:** "What do you do?"
>
> **Me**: "We excite audiences." (The hook)
>
> **Conversation Partner:** "How do you do that?"
>
> **Me:** "We're presentation coaches and hired gun speakers." (The reel)
>
> **Conversation Partner:** "What's a hired gun speaker."

You may have noticed my hook and reel are statements, not questions. So technically my hook and real can't be converted into traditional mind questions, because they are not questions. However, all I really have to do is acknowledge what my audience is thinking to make it work. After, "we excite audiences," I know my audience is confused. I just need to acknowledge their confusion. After my reel, I know they are wondering what a hired gun speaker is, so I acknowledge that.

Let's look at how my hook and reel can be converted to a spotlight moment.

"We excite audiences." - (Wait two second)

"You're probably wondering what that means." - (This will often be greeted by laughter from the group. Give them time to laugh.)

"We do this by being presentation coaches and hired gun speakers." - (Wait)

"Now, you're probably really confused. What's a hired gun speaker?" - (This statement may receive laughs too.)

"Let me tell you what a hired gun speaker is ..."

In this case, I am doing all the talking, but notice how it still felt like a conversation. By acknowledging what the group was thinking, I created a conversational feel. I also lighten up the mood of the room and tuned people in. Now they want to hear what I will say next. The opening is the secret to being successful. Get the opening right and you'll smoke the rest of your spotlight moment with ease.

As discussed in chapter 5, you can watch facial gestures while doing this. After I say "we excite audiences," and begin waiting, I will see people lower their eyebrows or raise their lips on one side of their mouths. These are the tale-tale signs of confusion. As soon as I see a number of these clues in the audience, I have waited long enough. With practice you will get better at spotting these subtle facial expressions too. This will allow you to time your speaking more effectively. Just like a good comedian, it's all in the timing. Keep working on it and you'll master the technique. Don't give up on the first try if you don't get stellar results right a way. If you were learning to play tennis and on your first swing you didn't get the ball over the net, you wouldn't just give up would you?

Let's look at another example.

> "We sell fifteen minute vacations." - (pause)

> "You might be wondering how we do that. When you get in one of our cars, you will be in paradise. Are you intrigued yet?" - (pause)

> "When was the last time you were in a Lincoln Town Car?"

In this example, you may have noticed the second sentence of the reel was a question. This is an effective method. The second question, "are you intrigued yet," acknowledges what the audience is thinking again. The more you can do this, the better.

Possibility #2: The show.

Entertain them right out of the shoot. This technique definitely takes planning and work, but it is so different than anything else out there, that you will really catch the attention of any networking group. The only good way to describe this technique is to give you an example.

> "I was giving a seminar a while back and in the break the CEO of a gravel and sand company came up to me and commented, 'all your information is great Cliff, but we just don't have the time or resources to work on our presentation skills.'
>
> 'Hmmm ... I see, so when is your next presentation?'
>
> 'At the national convention.'
>
> 'How many of your prospective customers will be there?'
>
> 'I would guess about 500.'
>
> 'If you improve your presentation skills just enough to get one more client out of that presentation, how much profit will your company make?'
>
> I watched his jaw drop as he said, 'five million dollars.'
>
> (Address the group), 'Do you have the time and resources NOT to work on YOUR presentation skills?'"

What I've done here is to put on a little mini-show. A short, and short is important, drama about my services. This will be so different than the guy just before me, and after me, that the contrast will stun everyone in the room. Now, I've got them.

I am going to put an asterisk on this technique right now. If you don't do this well, it will really backfire on you. To succeed with this method takes some speaking/story telling skills. This technique done poorly will get you attention, but probably not the type of attention you're looking for. I could write an entire book on just this subject, but that is way outside the scope of this book.

If you're already comfortable speaking, this technique maybe worth a try. If you need more information on how to pull this off, I would suggest that you purchase my six CD set, "Audience in the Palm - Speaking Coach in a Box." Pay special attention to the two discs "Story Telling For Business Parts 1 & 2." By applying the tips and secrets on these two discs, you can stop being a commercial and start being the show. I would love to supply you with the tips here, but there is just no good way to do this in print. You need to hear the audio examples. Obviously, this technique takes practice and training and the CD set is a great place to start.

Possibility #3: The testimonial.

There is no better salesperson for your company than a happy customer. Why not take advantage of this valuable marketing tool. This is probably the easiest one to implement, because you can read most of it. In fact, the secret to success is to read it from a piece of paper. This is how to properly execute this technique:

> Start out with, "I'd like to share something with you."

Pull out a piece of paper from your pocket or purse and read a testimonial from one of your clients. If you wear reading glasses, putting them on is even more dramatic and attention getting.

> "My company's profits soared after implementing your system ... blah, blah, blah ... signed Max Keller, vice-president of financial affairs, Acme Incorporated."

> End the testimonial with a comment like, "wouldn't it be great if we did this for your company?"

Now tell them how you do what you do. This can be very powerful if you have the right type of testimonial. Let's examine what makes a good testimonial. Of course a testimonial should be glowing, but you want it to be specific too. How did your product or service aid them in growing profits, finding customers, expanding their brand, etc. What did they specifically like about your product, customer service, facilities, etc. Who at your company treated them well. What model really met their needs. The more specific the better. Testimonials like, "your company was great. I loved working with you. It was a great experience," are useless. Something like, "we installed your A7 cooling system and our energy costs dropped 35% in just one month, you're saving us a fortune." That testimonial is better than gold.

Hopefully, you already have some great testimonials. If you don't, ask your customers to give you some. Most clients won't mind doing you a favor. In fact, many people will be flattered that you asked. It will make them feel important and show that you value their opinions and business. Another way to get testimonials, is to take note when your client says something great about you. Ask them for their permission to use the quote. Write down what they said as soon as possible so you don't forget.

Here is testimonial I received just by asking for it:

> "I'm a 4th year medical student currently interviewing for residency positions throughout the Mid-West. This period is famously one of the most stressful in the career of all medical students. However, Cliff's teachings have provided me a tremendous foundation of knowledge about the science of interpersonal communication. Being armed with this knowledge has increased my confidence allowing me to actually have fun at these interviews and has given me a clear advantage over other candidates. Thanks Cliff!"
> *Todd M. Hoffman, Medical Student Wayne State University*

This is a great testimonial. It's personal, it describes the benefit of my services, and it's specific. By the way, Todd was accepted into residency by his first choice hospital. Results like that are a great thing to add to the end of your spot light moment.

Another thing that makes a great testimonial is if it

comes from someone famous, note worthy, or important in your field. A testimonial like,

> "Wow, I can't believe how exciting my story became. Cliff made my speaking engagements easy."
> *Kristin Armstrong, 2008 Beijing Olympics Gold Medalist*

This testimonial is not very long or specific, but the star power of the person who gave you the quote really carries weight. Testimonials from presidents of big companies, political figures, celebrities, can really catch the attention of the group.

Whether the testimonial comes from someone famous or not, it's important to include their name and title at the end of the testimonial. By doing this, you not only add credibility, but it's also the right thing to do. Always honor the person who gave you the testimonial.

Whatever technique you decide to use, try not to be the first person in the group to talk. Part of the strength of these different methods is that it allows you to stand out from the crowd. Let them get good and bored and then be the breath of fresh air. Therefore, try not to sit just to the left or right of the person running the meeting, because you will increase you odds of being selected first.

Chapter #12
What to do after

Follow up after the initial meeting is important. Many people believe that all they have to do is meet people and then go back to the office and wait by the phone. This technique rarely works. If you meet an interesting prospective business relationship, you need to cultivate that relationship. Have you ever become good friends with someone on the first meeting? Where I have heard of this happening, I would suspect it's pretty rare. Business relationships, like friendships, take time.

The first step is to make a second contact. This is the point where many people mess things up. Their second contact is something along the lines of, "so how much do you want to buy and when can I expect your check?" This is not a very good idea. This will pretty much destroy any of the good vibes you created in your first meeting.

If you can follow up with valuable information instead, that is an awesome way to make a connection. Perhaps they want details on an event that is coming up. Maybe they want a phone number to a supplier that you use. You may know of an article you could fax them with business information they need. These are just a few examples of ways you can be of service to your contact. If during your next interaction you have information they need, you can be sure they will check out your message. An unread email, unheard phone message, or a ducked call might as well never have happened. Be useful to everyone you meet.

I belong to a number of associations. If during my first meeting I see an opportunity where one of these associations could be of service to my contact, I call them with membership information and/or interesting association sponsored events that may be coming up.

You need to think of networking as a spider web not as a rope. In business we are all connected to each other. If we all share resources, all businesses will do better. Even your competitors help you. To explain this concept, I want to reintroduce you to Bob Taylor, mentioned previously, who is the president of Taylor Guitars. I had a chance to interview Bob about ten years ago for a freelance article I was writing. I want to share the amazing answer he gave to this inquiry:

> "You're seen in the industry as someone who freely shares guitar building information with competitors. Do you see this as a positive or negative and why?"

> Bob replied, "I think it's positive. As they say, 'a rising tide floats all the boats'. Would you be writing this article if I was the only guy making guitars? No. How thick could an acoustic guitar magazine be if I was the only one making guitars and was successful at it. It would be very thin. I need to be part of an industry to survive. I can't be a

monopoly. I can't fuel a world of guitar players. I need all the controversy. I need people to hate our guitars. I need all of that. That's what makes it all work. Here is an example of what I'm talking about: I got really into building a home theater a few years ago. When I was building my theater I researched all this high end gear. Laser disk was the thing before DVD. I remember that Pioneer, who had 80% of the laser disk market, was constantly annoyed by having 80% of the market. They only wanted 20% of the market. They wanted Phillips and Sony to join. They realized that with them being the only player in the market, that the market would never survive and it didn't because other players didn't play. Now DVD is out and everyone is playing, and look what's happened."

I think Bob is right, and I hope you too will recognize the genius of his comments. Share the information you have. What you send out into the universe comes back ten fold. If we all work together, everybody wins.

Have you ever gone to an auto-mall? They have one in my town. An auto-mall is a section of town or maybe just one street where you have many different car dealerships in one place. It would seem, on the surface, that being so close to competitors would hurt their business, but these dealers have found just the opposite effect. By banding together they draw a lot of car buyers to their area. Sure they don't get all the sales, but they get a lot of people looking so they get their fair share of the bigger market.

Make yourself part of the business web. Share useful

information more than you share product flyers.

Sending product information to someone that has not requested it, is just more land fill materials. As mentioned in the last chapter, find out what your contacts need and supply it to them even if you don't sell it. This is how relationships are born.

I want to end this chapter by sharing with you an old but true rule of business. Never fax when you can email. Never email when you can write a letter. Never write a letter when you can call them on the phone. Never call them when you can see them in person.

After a recent business networking event, someone I met from a company called Golden Penguin took the time to send me a personally written note. Not a form letter, but a hand written note including comments about our conversation. That really stuck out in the crowd and I immediately responded with information about an association I thought would be useful to them.

Relationships are made face to face. Get personal with those in the business world around you.

Chapter #13
Final Thoughts

Well, there you have it. A simple way to energize your business networking. Now it's time to make a decision. Seventy-five percent of everything you learn is forgotten in the first forty-eight hours unless you practice. Create your Anti-Elevator Conversation today and find a networking event near you to start practicing. Do it today. Not in a while or next week or next quarter, do it today. Once you start using this technique and see the potential it has to improve your business, you will be hooked.

I have found that I can easily attend one or two networking events a week without spending much time looking for them. Here are few ideas for finding networking opportunities in your area:

> 1) Business calendars maintained by local newspapers, magazines, or city informational web-sites.

> 2) Chamber of Commerce. Most cities have one of these groups and they host and promote networking events.

> 3) Internet searches. Type in a search phrase that includes "Networking Event", your city, state, or

area and the year. You will be surprised how many hits you'll get.

4) Networking organizations like BNI. BNI is a large international networking group, but there are also many local groups as well. With a little investigative work, you can also find networking groups for women, small businesses, entrepreneurs, people in your industry, minorities, etc. The nice thing about these smaller networking groups, is that you have something in common right away.

5) Many cities have economic development groups that host or promote networking events.

6) And best of all, is to get information from people you meet at other networking events.

I'm hoping you and I will meet soon and I can hear your confusion hook. Until then, make as many relationships as you can.

Who is Cliff Suttle

Cliff Suttle is a sought after business speaker and lecturer. He is known for not only educating the audience, but delighting them at the same time. Realizing that he had a gift and a passion for business communications, Mr. Suttle founded and became the president of ExciteYourAudience.com a company dedicated to world class business/audience communications. This company not only supplies top of the game speaking talent for business events, but also teaches others how to be master communicators, convey their message and make it stick by hosting events that increase the company's bottom line.

Mr. Suttle is an awarding winning speaker, with over seventy championship titles to his credit. In the World Championships of Public Speaking, he has cracked into the top fifty in the world out of 25,000 contestants. He is the creator of the six-CD set, "Audience in the Palm - Speech Coach in a Box," which coaches people on different aspects of public speaking. He is the author of "The Anti-Elevator Speech," a book on effective business networking, and "Choose to Win - Lighting the Fire Within," a guide to personal motivation. Mr. Suttle is a successful freelance writer for print and multi-media publications and has been read internationally by millions.

Mr. Suttle gained over twenty years of solid executive business experience as CEO of Antler Software Technologies Inc, a custom software consulting firm. Antler Software Technologies supplied major software solutions for small businesses to Fortune 500 companies including General Motors, Ford Motor, IBM, Blue Cross/Blue Shield, Kodak, Xerox, and Metlife. Besides the usual CEO duties, Mr. Suttle was also the visual component of the company making presentations to business audiences from board of director meetings to large public events with thousand of attendees.

Mr. Suttle earned his B.S. in Management Information Sciences from the University of Michigan and is a certified Perk Performance Consultant.

ExciteYourAudience

Want to excite your audience? These products and services will help you do exactly that.

Hired Gun Speakers
 Corporate Presentations
 Corporate Sponsored Events
 Marketing Events
 Fund Raisers
 Promotional Events

Presentation Coaching
 Speech Writing
 Delivery Coaching
 Venue Set Up and Management
 Public Speaking Skills Training

Workshop and Keynotes
 Presentation Skills
 Motivational/Inspirational
 Networking
 Customer Service
 Business Communications Skills
 Parenting Skills & More

Products
 Books, CD's, and DVD's on a variety of topics

Contact Us Today, And Excite Your Next Audience! www.ExciteYourAudience.com

25977279R00046

Made in the USA
Middletown, DE
16 November 2015